THE COACHING COMPANION

Get the Most from Your Coaching Experience

Daniel Sheres, MPH, CLC
Carylynn Larson, PhD, ACC

2015
Alexandria, VA, USA

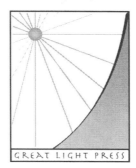

GREAT LIGHT PRESS

The Coaching Companion
Daniel Sheres and Carylynn Larson

Cover Design: Daniel Sheres
Copyeditor: Katie Aberbach

Although the authors have made every effort to ensure that the information in this book was correct at press time, the authors do not assume and hereby disclaim any liability to any party for any loss, damage, or disruption caused by errors or omissions, whether such errors or omissions result from negligence, accident, or any other cause.

ISBN: 978-0-9861579-1-2
Version 1.0

"Coaching unlocks potential in individuals, enabling them to see possibilities for their lives, their careers and their organizations. The Coaching Companion provides useful information, examples and ideas for application in a practical and usable book. A "must read" for anyone who wants to create the best coaching partnership."

– Pat Mathews, MA, RN, MCC
Leadership and Executive Coach
Program Director, Leadership Coaching Program,
Georgetown University
Founding Faculty Member, Institute for Transformational
Leadership, Georgetown University

"The Coaching Companion is a gem of a book and should be a must-read for anyone seeking to get the absolute most out of his/her coaching relationship. Cary and Daniel have done a wonderful job of incorporating real-life examples, years of firsthand coaching experience and a deep understanding of what makes us each truly unique - as well as the ways in which we are all utterly the same. Into these practical tips and valuable suggestions is woven an honesty and authenticity that is refreshing, solidly grounded and tremendously helpful. Highly, highly recommended!"

– Chalmers Brothers
Coach, Consultant, Speaker
Author of *Language & the Pursuit of Happiness*

"This book represents the culmination of years of work condensed into powerful insights that are perfect for anyone wanting to maximize a coaching experience. Whether you are just beginning or seek coaching regularly, you will benefit from the content and applications that Daniel and Carylynn have carefully thought out to ensure the successful integration of your experience."

– Brandon Moreno
Business Optimization Expert
Director of Talent Acquisition, Herbalife Inc.

Dedication

To all those dedicated to personal and professional growth
and to the coaches who support them in this mission.

Table of Contents

Foreword 1

Introduction 3
   How to Use This Book.................................... 4

Section One: The Growth Process 7
   Initiative 9
      Tip 1. Get Intentional................................... 9
      Tip 2. Visualize Goals.................................... 10
      Tip 3. Do Your Homework............................... 15
      Tip 4. Be Your Own Coach............................... 19
      Tip 5. Translate Insights to Action.................... 23
   Community..25
      Tip 6. Surround Yourself With Support.................... 25
      Tip 7. Find a Partner in the Process.................... 29
      Tip 8. Share What You Learn 32
      Tip 9. Give Them Time 35
   Momentum 39
      Tip 10. Trust Your Coach............................... 39
      Tip 11. Embrace Discomfort 41
      Tip 12. Beware of Competing Commitments 45
      Tip 13. Fear Not the Dark Corners 48
      Tip 14. Name Your Shame............................... 51

Self-Care **55**

    Tip 15. Honor Overwhelm....................................55

    Tip 16. Take Care of Yourself..............................59

    Tip 17. Exercise, and Make It Mindful.......................62

    Tip 18. Rejuvenate With Gratitude 65

Section Two: Growth Tactics....................................**67**

Focus **69**

    Tip 19. Come With a Clear Objective..........................69

    Tip 20. Eliminate Distractions 72

    Tip 21. Focus on Yourself.....................................74

    Tip 22. Start With an Accomplishment.........................80

Awareness..**83**

    Tip 23. Center Yourself......................................83

    Tip 24. Use Reminders to Break Patterns 87

    Tip 25. Keep a Development Log..............................90

    Tip 26. Remind Yourself With a Talisman 91

Priority **97**

    Tip 27. Clarify Expectations..................................97

    Tip 28. Protect Your Coaching................................99

    Tip 29. Schedule for Stability 102

    Tip 30. Blame it on Coaching................................106

Section Three: The Growth Mindset **111**

Perspective **113**

    Tip 31. Embrace 'Beginnerhood'..............................113

    Tip 32. Cultivate Curiosity..................................116

    Tip 33. Learn From Dead Ends 119

    Tip 34. Treat Inquiry as Action...............................122

Integration **125**

Tip 35. Allow Spillover 125

Tip 36. Fit Coaching Into Your Plan 129

Tip 37. Leverage Assessments 132

Tip 38. Use Language Strategically 135

Tip 39. Learn to Improvise 138

Acknowledgement **141**

Tip 40. Give Yourself Credit 141

Tip 41. Make a Personal Investment 143

Tip 42. Distinguish Between Failure and Mistake ... 147

Tip 43. Breathe Into Insights 151

Epilogue:
Applying These Principles to Everyday Life **155**

Acknowledgements **157**

About the Authors **159**

Daniel Sheres **161**

Carylynn Larson **165**

Foreword

During my career in various organizations – international, start-up, multinational and now higher education, I have seen firsthand the positive outcomes from coaching, particularly if you are ready for and open to the experience. There is also no better time to be coached; there are highly effective coaches in the United States and globally, with the ability to serve clients at different stages of their careers and their lives. Concurrently, organizations and individuals have a growing recognition of the benefits and engaging a coach is often part of the arc of a career.

As a human resources and leadership development professional, I have the opportunity to meet and engage coaches for leaders and for those aspiring to lead. In talking with coaches and clients before, during and after their engagements, it is clear that clients who benefited most are those who are open to the process and do the work needed during the engagement. With the right resources and effort, it's not difficult to find a good coach and there is no dearth of books and articles about how to become one. However, this book serves a special purpose – it is client-centric and will enable you to get the most out of your coaching engagement. If you and/or your institution are committing time and other resources, here is a guide that could allow you to get extraordinary results.

On a personal note, Cary and Daniel were in my coaching cohort in the Leadership Coaching program at Georgetown University. They both bring a wise and thoughtful approach to their practice as coaches, but more importantly, they are completely committed to their clients getting everything they want and more from their coaching engagements. It is truly a privilege to be a very small part of the journey that Cary and Daniel have been on during the writing of "The Coaching Companion".

Use this book; return to it and enjoy it.

Junie Nathani
Assistant Vice President, Leadership Resources
Georgetown University

Introduction

As professional coaches, we are constantly looking for ways to facilitate transformation in our clients. We have experienced firsthand the kind of radical changes possible when our clients take conscious control over their personal and professional development. The intention to develop oneself carries a great deal of power; when combined with coaching, there is almost no limit to what is possible. Whether you have hired a coach yourself, or your company has offered you one, the investment made in coaching is typically significant. We believe you should expect returns that greatly outweigh the costs of coaching. Our intention in writing this book is simple: to present essential tips that will help you get the most value possible out of the coaching process.

The tips presented in this book are the same tips we offer to our clients on a regular basis. They are not specific to any one type of person or coaching objective, and will be useful to you regardless of your personal development goals. Many of the tips herein are concepts that we have learned on the receiving end of coaching, and have subsequently incorporated into our work as coaches. Other tips are insights we've gained from working with certain clients. A few tips were brought to us by our clients -- insights they've gained for themselves and shared with us. Several of our tips are foundational to coaching; to overlook them would be to compromise the coaching engagement. If you are new to coaching, these tips will help you to get started with some of the tried-and-true principles we, ourselves, adhere to. If you have experience working with a coach, these tips will serve as useful reminders that the value that we receive depends largely on our own approach to the process.

Although we have presented these tips in the context of coaching, many of them will be useful to anyone who seeks to advance in life. We hope this volume is something that you carry with you throughout your coaching journey.

How to Use This Book

The Coaching Companion is organized in three sections: The Growth Process, Growth Tactics, and The Growth Mindset. For each section, we have several thematic chapters, and within each chapter, you will find a handful of tips for getting the most from your coaching engagement. You may choose to read sequentially, and you may also find it helpful to reference the tips by thematic area. For example, when you are struggling to make coaching a priority amidst other demands on your time, you may find the tips under "Priority" particularly beneficial.

Each tip includes an application section. These application sections invite you to explore the relevance of the tip to your own development process and will help you think creatively about how to integrate the tip into your own life.

Many tips also include stories from real-life clients with whom we have worked. Their names and company names have been changed or left out entirely to honor our confidentiality agreements. These stories will help you to see both the context for the advice, and how others who may be facing similar challenges have applied each tip.

It is our sincere hope that the tips offered in this book speed up your progress and help to make your experience working with a coach as meaningful and valuable as possible.

To your success,

Daniel and Carylynn

Section One:
The Growth Process

Initiative

Tip 1. Get Intentional

"Intentional living is the art of making our own choices before others' choices make us."
— Richie Norton

Coaching invites you to be intentional. The more intentional you are, the more opportunities you'll find to practice the skills you are learning. One powerful way to become more intentional is to connect with largely unconscious actions such as breathing and eating—to bring these actions into our consciousness. When we're intentional about breathing, we expand our capacity to interrupt automatic thoughts and to calm ourselves. When we're intentional about eating, we strengthen our mind-body connection; we become more attuned to hunger and fullness cues, emotional and physiological cravings, taste and smell. The practice of being intentional about breathing and eating is a powerful reminder to be intentional in other domains of self-awareness.

Application

For at least one meal per day for one week, be intentional about what and how you eat. Start by paying attention to your hunger cues. When you feel hunger coming on, ask yourself what your body is asking you to eat. Intentionally seek to fulfill your body's request. As you eat, reflect on how the food is meeting your needs—both physically and emotionally. Pay attention to fullness cues. Pay attention to your decision to stop eating; sit with your fullness. If this is difficult for you, repeat the process often. Don't judge yourself; rather, be reflective and mindful. After a week of this practice, reflect on whether your intentions around breathing and/or eating have shifted.

Notes

Tip 2. Visualize Goals

"Man can only see what he sees himself receiving."
— Florence Scovel Shinn

There are countless examples of the power that visualization can have on goal accomplishment. To visualize a goal is to make it real in our mind's eye. Gymnasts visualize their routine so intimately that they can feel each movement of their body before beginning; runners visualize a race in advance, feeling the adrenaline as they rush off the starting line and noticing the last ounce of energy drain as they reach for the tape.

As these examples demonstrate, it is not enough to visualize the goal itself; rather, we must visualize *the process* of accomplishing that goal. The gymnast does not simply visualize himself on the medal stand. The runner does not only visualize herself crossing the finish line. In order to maximize the power of visualization, we must visualize ourselves in the process of goal accomplishment.

Visualization also helps us to focus our energy on that big goal that we're reaching for. When we focus on even two or three long-term goals, we often find that we make moderate progress at best. Moderate progress rarely produces the shift we hope to see, and is therefore only modestly motivating. By comparison, when we focus intently on only one big goal, we make remarkable, notable progress in that area. When we make a real shift, others notice, and the acknowledgement we receive creates momentum that helps to fuel the next goal.

Application

Select one major goal for your coaching engagement. Visualize yourself accomplishing this goal, and then move backwards from that moment until today. Visualize the conversations you will need to have. Visualize both the support and resistance likely to come from others. Visualize conversations that are likely to be difficult for you and managing the discomfort of an encounter you'd rather avoid.

To help you articulate your vision by leveraging the metaphorical power of imagery, create a vision board, a space where you display words and/or images that represent what you want to have, do, or be. Find words and pictures that appeal to you that represent something that you want, or want more of, in your life. Place these on or around a large sheet of paper or poster board. Once you have pictures and words that appeal to you, take a step back and ask yourself, "What is the essence of my board?"

Notes

Tip 3. Do Your Homework

"Twenty years from now you will be more disappointed by the things you didn't do than by the ones you did."
— H. Jackson Brown, Jr.

Most of the growth experienced in the coaching process happens between coaching sessions. At the end of each session, we are often given or asked to identify an exercise designed to build self-awareness, promote embodiment of a new skill, or challenge us to step outside our comfort zone. It is crucial for us to do our exercises. If we set a goal to have better posture, standing tall for one hour every other week won't help much. Rather, to achieve lasting improvement in our posture, we will need to bring awareness to our posture and make adjustments many times a day.

Let's consider for a moment the factors that get in the way of doing our exercises. The most common reason that we fail to follow through on our exercises is that we never fully committed to them in the first place. We need to be discerning in what we agree to. If our coach suggests an exercise that we know we will not do, we can say "no." We can also suggest an alternative exercise that we are willing to do. We're most likely to neglect exercises when we are either overwhelmed or underwhelmed by the nature of the

15

exercise we chose or that our coach picked out for us. When we're feeling overwhelmed by what we've committed to do, we can make just one simple shift in our behavior. Alternatively, when we find ourselves only motivated by big leaps, we can challenge ourselves to do something heroic or vastly different.

Coach: What can you commit to doing over the next week in order to become a better observer of how others respond to you?

Client: I'm not sure—what would you suggest?

Coach: Do you take notes during meetings?

Client: Most of the time, yes.

Coach: As you take notes, could you record not only what was said, but also how the person is communicating? Could you note, for example, their tone of voice?

Client: Yes, I can do that.

Coach: What could you note in addition to tone of voice?

Client: I could note how I think they're feeling —frustrated, pleased, bored, excited, etc.

Coach: Sounds good. Can you commit to doing this in every work meeting you have for the next week?

Client: Yes, I can commit to that.

Application

Choose a way to hold yourself accountable for completing any exercises that you commit to doing. Consider enlisting a colleague or friend to help you honor your commitment. Communicate this to your coach.

Notes

Tip 4. Be Your Own Coach

Coaching provides an opportunity to make the growth experience uniquely ours. Good coaches can adjust to the pace, personality, and learning style of their clients, but they are not mind readers. When our coach offers us an idea or a framework, we can take the opportunity to consider how we can best tailor it to fit our unique position and personality. This does not mean that if we don't like a framework or an assignment that our coach gave us, we can just create our own framework or do our own thing. There's a fine line here. If we only adopt frameworks that conform to our existing beliefs, and if we customize our coaching activities to fit too closely with our personality and preferences, we risk staying in our comfort zone and learning nothing new.

The key to successfully tailoring our coaching experience to ourselves is to begin to be our own coach. Most coaches want to help their clients build the capacity to coach themselves. There is a method behind the coaching approach, and it should be no secret. We can ask our coach how and why he or she has recommended a certain approach, tool, or process.

We don't have to rely on our coach to call us out on making something too easy; we can do an honest assessment and let our coach know what would be a real challenge for us. We can recognize when our coach's style isn't serving us well and request an adjustment. We don't have to wait for our coach to ask us hard questions, either. We can even offer a question that our coach should ask us —perhaps one that we are terrified of being asked. When we actively participate in crafting our coaching experience, we exponentially increase the capacity for meaningful outcomes.

Susan, an executive in a fast-paced consulting firm, quickly realized that her coach both asked a lot of questions and allowed a great deal of silence in their conversations. Following one coaching session, Susan wondered why she didn't take time to think outside her coaching conversations. In that moment, she realized that she could give herself the gift of time. Susan began asking herself questions, slowing down when she landed on a good one and reflecting on that question until she gained insight. She shared these activities with her coach, and asked her coach to hold her accountable for them. She also asked her coach to hold her accountable for asking herself deeper questions—more "why" questions as opposed to "what" questions.

Application

Identify one way your coach interacts with you that you can apply in your own life.

Consider these questions:

- What about the coaching process or your coach's style would you like to change?
- What about the coaching process or your coach's style is working well?
- What request(s) might you make of your coach to ensure the process is optimal for you, your personality, and/or your learning style?

Notes

Tip 5. Translate Insights to Action

"A good composer borrows, a great composer steals."
– Jaco Pastorius

The "Eureka!" moments we experience in dialogue with our coach are exciting and to be expected. A risk of coaching is that we emerge with many insights and very little transformation. For example, realizing that we are not as influential as we would like to be isn't the same as *being* or *becoming* influential. Translating our insights into meaningful and relevant action allows us to embody the change that we desire for ourselves.

At times, it feels overwhelming to translate insight into action. There will be insights that seem so big that no action appears available to us. In such cases, it is helpful to first embody an insight in a very simple situation, and then challenge ourselves to take action on that insight in progressively more complex scenarios. By gently moving into action on a given insight, we can reduce resistance to change and generate momentum to practice at higher and higher levels.

Application

Identify one insight that you gained in a coaching conversation. Make a list of ways that you can better express this insight through your actions. Share your list with your coach and discuss ways that you can translate this insight into action, starting with easy examples and working your way up to situations in which you would find it difficult, perhaps even a little scary. Notice as it becomes easier and easier to take action with practice.

Notes

Community

Tip 6. Surround Yourself With Support

"You are not alone."
– Alcoholics Anonymous mantra

Our beliefs and behaviors are heavily influenced by the people present in our social environment. Our social environment can hold more sway over our behaviors, decisions, and opportunities than any other factor. The people who surround us either support or hinder our progress of growth and transformation. This is especially true during times of transition, when we need all the energy we can muster to face challenges and secure new opportunities. In order to carry the energy we gain in our coaching conversation into everyday life, we need to surround ourselves with supportive people.

When Daniel first went out on his own as a consultant, he realized very quickly that he was surrounded by risk-averse people. Some of them were among his parents, friends, and colleagues. He had to determine who was giving him good advice and who was simply expressing their own fears. It was at this point that he consciously chose to balance the risk-averse influences with the bold attitudes of other entrepreneurs. He joined a networking group for entrepreneurs and began limiting the time he spent with his risk-averse family, friends, and colleagues. As a result, Daniel's social environment became more supportive of his endeavors, giving him more energy, optimism, and courage to move forward.

Supportive people come in many forms. Just as having a workout buddy can help us stay on track at the gym, forming an accountability partnership can be an invaluable tool for sustaining momentum through our coaching activities. Similarly, engaging with a community of other growth-minded individuals can help to counteract the tendency we all have to think we are alone in facing our challenges. By maximizing our time with supportive people within our social network and expanding our network to include a dedicated transformational community, we can maximize the growth that we experience in-between our formal coaching sessions.

Surrounding ourselves with support also involves limiting our exposure to those who hold us back. People who hinder our progress generally come in one of two forms: they simply reinforce habitual behaviors we now want to leave behind, or worse, they are overtly cynical. We may discover that we unconsciously associate certain people with our status quo or our past, and that being around these people now feels like giving up on our goals. Cynicism is particularly draining and has been shown to tax us emotionally, physically, and in our relationships. Cynicism is easily recognized by a scornful and pessimistic attitude. The last thing we need when we're investing in our own growth and transformation is to be around those who exhaust us, who scorn our growth, and who doubt our capacity to accomplish our goals.

Application

Make a list of the people with whom you interact on a daily, weekly, and monthly basis. Put a (+) next to each person who has a positive influence on your growth and development, and a (-) next to each person who has a negative influence on your growth. Talk to your coach about how you can limit your exposure to negative influences and maximize your exposure to positive ones.

Find an accountability partner, and/or join a transformational community. In either case, be sure to share your coaching objectives.

Notes

Tip 7. Find a Partner in the Process

The majority of the growth experienced in the coaching process will occur in-between the formal coaching sessions. Just as having a "workout buddy" can help us to stay on track at the gym, finding someone to partner with in the process of coaching can be an invaluable tool for sustaining momentum. It can also be very rewarding to support someone else through his or her own transformation.

Shortly after beginning his executive coaching engagement, Joshua formed an accountability partnership with his friend John, who was also working with a coach at another company. For six months, they committed to sending each other an email at the end of each day listing the actions, inquiries, and observational practices they undertook that day. Additionally, they agreed to have a one-hour call each week when they would have the opportunity to talk about the gains and challenges they had experienced. Having a partner in the process was encouraging to Joshua, and even though he and John were working with their coaches to achieve different objectives, he found there were many commonalities between them.

Whether or not partners share similar objectives for their respective coaching engagements does not matter. This partnership can take many forms, from informal period meetings to more formal arrangements designed to help with specific aspects of the process, such as holding each other accountable to critical action steps. Simply meeting from time to time to discuss the growth process can be helpful. We can often double the value of our coaching experience by exposing ourselves to the coaching process of our partner.

Application

Identify a friend or colleague who you can talk to from time to time about the coaching experience and who might be willing to help hold you accountable to the commitments you make as part of your coaching process. Consider asking your coach if he or she has any other clients who might be willing to serve in this capacity.

In forming your partnership, be sure to come to agreement on the following:
- Overall duration of the partnership, frequency and duration of the interactions
- Communication protocols (email, phone, text, in-person, etc.)
- What you will and will not hold one another accountable for
- How you would like to handle situations in which one of you has missed a commitment
- How you would like to handle changes in the structure of the partnership (timing, style of interaction, etc.)

Notes

Tip 8. Share What You Learn

"We teach what we need to learn."
– Anonymous

For many people, teaching what we learn is one of the best ways to ensure that what we learn is not forgotten. Sharing helps us process concepts at a deeper level by challenging us to make the value of our knowledge and experiences accessible to others. It also helps us to recognize gaps in our own understanding and search for meaning to fill those gaps. Sharing often evokes questions that lead us back into sequentially deeper levels of self-inquiry.

Because coaching is a deeply personal experience, we often overlook opportunities to share what we learn. We may not want to share specifically what we're learning about ourselves. It helps to remember that we can share parts of our coaching process without sharing any personal details at all. For example, we can share a question that had a powerful impact on us without any need to go into *how* the question impacted us.

At the end of every workshop he runs, Daniel asks each participant to identify two ideas that he or she found interesting, and to share those ideas with three people who were not in attendance. This gives participants the opportunity to attempt to put the lessons learned into their own language, building a deeper level of understanding among the participants and extending the reach of the lessons beyond the workshop audience.

When we share tools and techniques that we have found helpful, it usually serves us as much, if not more, than the person with whom we share.

Application

List a few of the lessons that you've learned through your coaching engagement. Identify three people who could also benefit from learning these lessons. Share what you've learned with each of them.

Notes

Tip 9. Give Them Time

When we're engaged in coaching, we have front row seats to the change process. We develop in ways we never thought possible: Mediocre managers become great managers; poor communicators become sought-after public speakers; shy individuals become fearless; the list goes on and on. Coaching tends to speed up the development process beyond what our friends, family, and colleagues are accustomed to or even thought possible.

For those around us—and particularly for those close to us —the degree of change in us can be confusing. Many of us don't change much at all, leading to an expectation that others maintain that same consistency of thinking and behavior. People even enjoy and feel validated when their assumptions about others hold true. It takes time and consistency in our new behaviors for the assumptions that others make about us to fall away in light of new information. This means that we need to be consistent with our new behaviors, patient with others, and as best we can, seek validation from within and from those who have a heightened capacity to perceive growth.

Robert had developed a reputation as a "bull in a china shop," particularly when engaging with managers of other functional units. Rather than sharing ideas and asking his peers what they thought, Robert would declare his plans as undisputable facts. Rather than seeking to build consensus among his peers, Robert would move forward regardless of others' opinions. Through coaching, Robert began to realize that while his bullish approach had contributed to his success thus far, it would hold him back from senior management roles. Robert made a sincere commitment to change, and from that point on, he began asking more questions and taking others' perspectives into account.

After a few months of adopting these new behaviors, Robert expected his colleagues to acknowledge him as a collaborative business partner. Instead, Robert's colleagues still described him as bullish and inconsiderate. Rather than attributing Robert's new behaviors to a change in him, they assumed his behavior was an anomaly, or worse, that he would undermine their authority in some other way. For Robert, the challenge was to continue seeking collaborative business relationships even when his colleagues remained wary of him.

Application

Identify one or two assumptions people make about you that you would like to see shift as a result of coaching. Whether or not these assumptions are still true, reflect on how you can allow them to remain. Work with your coach to identify when to gather feedback on the change that others have seen in you.

Notes

Momentum

Tip 10. Trust Your Coach

"Trust is the glue of life."
– Stephen R. Covey

The coaching relationship only works in the context of trust. Once we decide that a coach is right for us, we need to extend trust to him or her. The act of extending trust is more difficult for some than others. Some of us tend to extend trust without proof of trustworthiness. We trust instinctively, unless and until those we trust betray us. Others tend to reserve trust for those who prove themselves as trustworthy.

Identifying where we lie on this spectrum of extending trust can help us understand how to build and retain trust with our coach. Those who trust without proof of trustworthiness can proactively consider and communicate expectations, for example, around confidentiality and anonymity. Those who need their coach to prove his or her trustworthiness can ask questions to accelerate the vetting process and to build rapport. Regardless of the way that we establish and maintain trust in our relationships, it is imperative to establish as much trust as possible in the beginning of our coaching engagements.

Lucy is an inherently trusting person. She naturally gives people the benefit of the doubt and believes that with rare exception, people have good intentions even when they make mistakes. Lucy trusted her coach because she had no reason not to, and so it never occurred to ask her coach if he or she was coaching anyone else in her organization.

A few months went by before Lucy discovered her coach was also working with a colleague from another division—not just any colleague, but the person with whom Lucy had the most difficulty. Lucy's trust in her coach was threatened by this revelation. She feared that her coach would not be able to coach them both without revealing the privileged content of their discussions.

If Lucy had let this fear manifest as a lack of trust in her coach's ability to maintain confidentiality, she could have lost the ability to address issues she had with this coworker. Instead Lucy shared her concern, and her coach was able to alleviate her fears. Lucy learned that an important component of trust is to come to a common understanding about which information is privileged and which may be shared.

Application

Reflect on how you form trusting relationships with others, considering both your professional and personal relationships. Share any insights you gain from this reflection activity with your coach.

Notes

Tip 11. Embrace Discomfort

Coaches often challenge us to leave our comfort zone. By definition, when we leave our comfort zone we experience discomfort. We can feel anxious or fearful, even resentful or angry. The emotions we experience are not right or wrong, good or bad—they are simply a natural part of the change process. They are to be expected. Rather than resist them, we can embrace them as a signal of growth.

We can't predict the specific emotional experiences that will arise during our coaching process, but we can be certain that emotions will be a part of the experience. When we allow emotions to rise to the surface, we create an opportunity to work with them. Emotional energy can hold us back or propel us forward. What we do with these emotions will impact how we respond to coaching challenges. Rather than avoid them or become paralyzed by them, we can begin to see our emotional reactions as a natural part of the process.

Putting emotions in the context of change helps us shift our focus away from emotions and back to the transformation process itself. By reminding ourselves periodically that these feelings are to be expected, we can better sustain motivation past the point of discomfort.

Application

The quickest way to experience how we feel when we leave our comfort zone is to hold our breath. For a brief few seconds, simply close your eyes and hold your breath. Notice any sensations in the body. Begin to identify the commonalities between what you experience when you hold your breath and the discomfort that you feel when you step outside your comfort zone. Talk to your coach about both the mental and physical aspects of the experience: the thoughts and stories that come to mind, and the sensory experience of discomfort. Identify a way that you can reframe discomfort so that it will help propel you forward toward growth.

Notes

Tip 12. Beware of Competing Commitments

We may be truly committed to our coaching goals and yet find it difficult to take the actions required to achieve them. Change tends to induce a dynamic tension between the attraction of our objectives and the attachments we have to "the way things are." When we experience this tension, we can to look for competing commitments hiding in the shadows and hindering our progress.

John served as a senior technician at a large manufacturing firm for over ten years before he was promoted to a management position that put him in charge of his teammates. John was excited that his organization recognized his leadership potential and wanted to excel at this new level of responsibility. A year after his promotion, however, John's boss discovered that the productivity on John's team had been steadily declining.

In his work with a leadership coach, John discovered a key commitment that competed with his desire to excel as a manager: John strongly valued being "one of the guys" and was afraid that fully adopting the management role would threaten the friendships that he has developed over the years. As a manager, John was inclined to be more demanding of his staff. Yet, as "one of the guys," John found this difficult. John's leadership capacity improved greatly by identifying and addressing these competing commitments.

As John's story shows, competing commitments sabotage our progress towards goals. When we take the time to identify our competing commitments, we create the opportunity to address them.

Application

Identify one goal that you have repeatedly set, yet not made much progress toward accomplishing. With this goal in mind, reflect on the following questions and share your thoughts with your coach: Is there anything about accomplishing this goal that scares you? What values do you hold that may support or hinder the possibility of achieving that goal?

Notes

Tip 13. Fear Not the Dark Corners

"The curious paradox is this - Once I accept myself as I am, then I can change."
– Carl Rogers

The conditions of our life are the result of our dominant patterns of thinking and behavior. While we are all aware of this to some extent, the relationship between the way we think and behave and the results we achieve is, to a large extent, hidden from our direct awareness. Most of us operate by reflex, a result of our conditioned behaviors. The coaching process is designed to reveal these behaviors, so that they may be examined. By bringing these hidden aspects of our personality to the surface, we are presented with the opportunity to take a new measure of control by operating from a place of choice.

Without shining a light on these patterns through self-reflection and contemplation, they will most likely continue to remain in the shadows. Oftentimes, these patterns are surprising. We learn things about ourselves that we simply didn't know before. Other times, we have had an intuition, or have been given feedback on an aspect of our personalities that we would rather avoid than address. Many of us can identify a few topics that we don't want to discuss with anyone, let alone our coach.

Much of what we gain from the coaching process depends on our willingness to leave all topics of discussion on the table. Coaching conversations have a tendency to bring up old (or new) baggage, and almost everyone has a topic of conversation that we will do everything in our power to avoid. We've stashed parts of ourselves away in boxes from our past, in hopes that they will be lost and forgotten. Rather than accepting these unacknowledged parts of our selves, we often reject them, push them away, and hope they never reappear. We like to think that we can write a different future for ourselves without accepting our past or even our present.

The danger of leaving these boxes untouched is that they often contain the very barriers to progress that we need to address. It takes courage to look into the dark corners of our life. When we are willing to leave as many topics as possible on the table for discussion, we increase the likelihood that we will find opportunities for growth.

From time to time, we may discover aspects of our personality that we simply do not want to accept. When we do, we can challenge ourselves to accept them as a part of who we are, or perhaps, who we were. Acceptance in this sense is not resignation but rather the means by which we may take ownership of our story—past, present, and future. By fully accepting who we have been, where we have been, and how we have acted, we can truly understand and accept where we are at this present moment. This radical self-acceptance might be thought of as "picking up the pen."

And only in the present moment can we author a different future for ourselves.

Note: In instances where we have experienced trauma or intense pain, we may find that it's only appropriate to address these topics with a professional therapist. Many of us have found that coaching led us to therapy, and many who search through their past with therapy also search for their future with a coach.

For twenty years, Sharon was a highly accomplished human resources executive. In recent years, she found herself more exhausted and overwhelmed by her position than usual. She decided to leave her position and work with a career coach to identify new paths forward.

After Sharon took standard career path assessments and put her resume together, her coach asked her about her social life. Initially, Sharon resisted this topic, seeing it as irrelevant to her stated objective. The truth was, however, her career had so dominated her life that her social life had become nonexistent. As important as her career was to her, Sharon realized that she would be better able to handle the stress of management if she could find better balance between work and her social life. If Sharon had been unwilling to shine a light in this dark corner, she could easily have found herself in a new position, yet feeling exactly the way she did before.

Application

Take a few moments to scan your life, from your earliest memories to your most recent. Which sections did you "skim over?" What is it about those times of your life that you are unwilling to face?

Identify one aspect of yourself that you need to accept—fully and without reservation—today.

Notes

Tip 14. Name Your Shame

"To name it is to tame it."
– Jeremy Sherman

Learning often occurs when we step outside our comfort zone—when we put ourselves out there and try new things. The challenge in doing so is that this is also the time when we are most vulnerable to the judgment of others. The feeling of vulnerability can be overwhelming, and at times it can compromise opportunities to learn. Our memories of instances when we stepped outside our comfort zone, only to have others' reactions make us feel like an outsider or a failure, can still hijack us today. Many of us learned not to put ourselves out there again. We can, however, learn to handle these "outside the box" experiences differently.

The key is to "name our shame"—to put words to the experience, ideally in that very moment. We need to name it to ourselves and also to others who will offer empathy and support. We can often add a little humor and share with complete strangers. By acknowledging and communicating our feelings of vulnerability, the judgments of others lose their ability to send us into a spiral of self-condemnation.

Sian wanted to lead his staff in a team-building activity. Although he worried that his team would think the activity was a waste of time, Sian envisioned standing firm and leading the group with confidence. When the time came, however, his worries came flooding back and he stammered through his explanation of the activity. He felt awkward, and his staff, in turn, felt awkward. The group went through the motions of the activity hesitantly, and without enthusiasm. Sian left the meeting feeling angry and ashamed. He wanted to hide from his staff and pretend that the exercise never happened. When his coach asked how the activity went, Sian cringed.

It is quite possible that the memory of this event could have triggered this shame response for years to come. Instead, Sian worked with his coach to put words to his vulnerability. As he shared the story and his coach empathized, Sian felt the weight of shame lifting. He chuckled. He shared his experience with his son, who laughed with him. He even shared his experience with his team prior to trying out a different team-building activity.

Application

Recall a memory you'd rather not relive—it need not be a traumatic event, but merely one that brought up feelings of shame or self-doubt. Imagine, for a moment, that the story happened to someone else. What words would you use to describe the experience of this memory? Consider sharing these words with your coach and using this process as a way to learn how to better transcend difficult experiences.

Notes

Self-Care

Tip 15. Honor Overwhelm

"Sometimes when you're overwhelmed by a situation - when you're in the darkest of darkness - that's when your priorities are reordered."
– Phoebe Snow

The coaching process can be overwhelming at times. We may try something new, only to be overtaken by self-doubt. We may experience the unexpected when we're not in the best frame of mind to handle it or to reflect on our response. At these times, it may be necessary to honor the feeling of being overwhelmed by submitting ourselves to it—by allowing ourselves to feel this way and by giving ourselves time to recover. At other times, we can anticipate becoming overwhelmed and plan around it. For example, if we know that our ability to make decisions is compromised by the end of the day, we might consciously avoid making big decisions after a certain time. 3:00 p.m. handled so many issues that his ability to see situations clearly could be compromised.

Jorge, a CEO of a not-for-profit organization, is often overwhelmed by the various demands on his time. When Jorge began working with a coach, he found himself nearly paralyzed by the addition of biweekly coaching sessions and the requirement to take certain actions in between sessions. After a few weeks, Jorge realized that the feeling of being overwhelmed brought on by coaching sessions was the same feeling that he experienced when he pursued any new, challenging opportunity. Instead of allowing overwhelming thoughts and feelings to compromise his coaching experience, Jorge learned to find peace in the midst of overwhelm. Jorge learned to schedule coaching meetings in the morning so that he could engage with a fresh and open mind.

There will always be times when we can't predict or prepare for the feeling of being overwhelmed at the very moment it hits. In these times, we need something to calm us, to remind us of all that is good and right in our life. We can shift back into an energized state of mind through the use of mood shifters. A mood shifter can be an inside joke, a favorite song, a picture of a loved one, or anything else that makes you smile or laugh.

Application

Reflect on what overwhelms you. Share your insights with your coach and discuss ways you can resolve this overwhelmed feeling, both in the moment and ahead of time.

Identify at least one mood shifter—something that is guaranteed to make you smile—and keep it at hand. For example, you could:

- Keep a special photo album on your phone that you can open whenever you're feeling down.
- Have a short list of songs at the ready on your phone that you can play to bring you joy in a tough moment.
- Save a clip of your favorite comedian on your phone and watch it to feel better.

Notes

Tip 16. Take Care of Yourself

"If there is no stillness, there is no silence.
If there is no silence, there is no insight.
If there is no insight, there is no clarity."
– Tenzin Priyadarshi

Trying new activities and attempting to see situations differently can be physically taxing—literally. Neuroscientists are now studying the ways our brain changes during times of transition, as old neural networks die and new ones are formed. We need to take care of our physical selves just as much as we need to take care of our psychological selves.

Exercise helps us sustain energy throughout the day. Sometimes the exhaustion that we experience is simply the result of poor hydration and/or nutrition. When we climb mountains and run marathons, we have to drink before we feel thirsty and eat before we feel hungry, so as to sustain the energy necessary to keep moving forward. If we find ourselves hungry or thirsty, it is already too late, and we will lose valuable time as our bodies recover. Personal development is much like mountain climbing and marathon running.

We can give ourselves the gift of rest after each coaching session. If we find ourselves too tired to enter fully into our coaching sessions, we can plan for extra rest and less activity in the hours leading up to our sessions.

Tara left the office for a walk every day. Olya set aside five minutes to meditate after lunch. Mike parked in a lot several blocks away from his office so that he could walk to and from work. Sylvia came into work an hour late on the days when she had a coaching session. Eric blocked off an hour after each coaching session to walk and reflect on the conversation. Susan filled a large container of water at the beginning of each day and committed to finishing it before dinner. Sara worked with a dietician to fuel her body more consistently. Each of these clients found one way to take care of themselves—a reminder that while they can't fully control their energy, they can take action to manage it.

Application

Open your calendar. On the days when you have scheduled coaching sessions, find one way to give yourself a break before and after your session.

Notes

Tip 17. Exercise, and Make It Mindful

Our body provides useful information and feedback on the degree to which our goals and experiences in pursuit of those goals resonate with us. The body is a wonderful barometer that signals how we feel about people, ideas, opportunities, and challenges. The body can signal to us whether or not a person, idea, or opportunity really resonates with us. It is through the experience of the body that we know we are relaxed or anxious, confident or overwhelmed, satisfied or dissatisfied, and so on.

Integrating a body-based practice is extremely helpful in times of transition. Exercise itself helps us process emotions, and has been proven to be as effective as psychotherapy in warding off bad moods and helping us sustain energy throughout the day. We can move beyond these straightforward health benefits by bringing an element of mindfulness to our practice. As we refine our awareness of the experience of change in our body, we build a foundation for resilience. Activities that have an explicit mindfulness component, such as martial arts and yoga, are easier for those of us who are new to the concept of integrating mindfulness and exercise.

Application

Just prior to your next workout, take a few moments to become more aware of the state of your body. Beginning with a couple of simple breaths, begin to scan your body for tension. Direct your attention to your feet and toes, and then to your knees and calves, thighs and hips, belly, chest and back, arms and hands, neck and shoulders, and finally jaw, forehead, and scalp. Pause at each part to simply notice the sensations. Then ask yourself, "Could I welcome any tension in my feet and toes? And could I also welcome relaxation in my feet and toes?" Continue alternating back and forth between these questions as you direct your attention to the various parts of your body. Repeat this process after the workout, noting any and all changes, significant or subtle.

Notes

Tip 18. Rejuvenate With Gratitude

"The struggle ends when gratitude begins."
– Neale Donald Walsch

Coaching can be concurrently invigorating and exhausting. It requires a huge amount of energy. Sometimes, coaching makes us think so hard our head hurts. Coaching can lead us to break through layers of resistance. Coaching can invite us to work through strong feelings. We can be challenged by assignments. All of these activities can be draining. The ongoing coaching process pushes us even further, inviting and even requiring us to integrate self-reflection and self-development activities into everyday work and personal activities. When the rush of energy and activity dissipates, we can find ourselves exhausted. To get the most out of our coaching engagement, we need to protect our energy. We can do this by remembering to recharge before we feel the need to do so, well before we are exhausted.

There are many ways to get ahead of exhaustion. We can start each and every day with an accomplishment. When we start our day by getting something done, we are much more likely to get a lot done. We can take the pressure off ourselves and infuse a little fun into our day. We can connect with gratitude.

Application

Find a journal or notepad, write "Gratitudes" on the front cover, and keep it next to your bed. On the first night, turn to the first page and allow yourself to write down a few things you are grateful for. When you stop writing, take a moment to let your gratitudes fill you up. When you get up the next morning, put your notebook by your pillow as a reminder for the following night. Do this every night for a month.

Notes

Section Two:
Growth Tactics

Focus

Tip 19. Come With a Clear Objective

"If you don't know where you're going, any road will get you there."
– Lewis Carroll

Growth and personal transformation come through being clear about what we want. Just as the act of setting a goal increases the probability that we will achieve our goal, knowing what we want to get out of a conversation greatly increases the probability that we will get what we want out of the conversation. Sometimes we don't want anything specific out of a conversation; we often talk to fill silence, to be polite, to share our thoughts, and to respond to others.

Coaching works best through conversations that are not just interesting, but also purposeful. When we come to a coaching conversation without a clear sense of what we want from it, our coach will have to take time to help us figure it out. If we can identify what we want from a given session before meeting with our coach, we can move more quickly into purposeful dialogue. Otherwise, our coaching session may be fully dedicated to gaining clarity on what we want.

Mike, a senior manager with over thirty years of experience in his field, found it difficult to know what he should get out of any given coaching session. Although he had set clear goals for the coaching engagement as a whole, he often asked his coach, "What do you think I should get out of today's session?" Mike's coach sometimes suggested topics, but (to Mike's dismay) still asked Mike what a successful outcome of the day's meeting would be. Often, Mike could not articulate what he wanted until the very end of the coaching conversation. To his surprise, once he identified a goal for the coaching session, Mike discovered that the conversation became more focused and productive. Over time, Mike learned what could be accomplished during coaching conversations, and started to come to each session with a specific goal.

Application
Finish this statement prior to each coaching session: By the end of this coaching conversation, I will be: _____.

Notes

Tip 20. Eliminate Distractions

The power of coaching comes through the invitation for us, as the client, to be completely open and honest with our coach. Distractions detract from our ability to focus, think, feel, and fully engage with our coach. Finding a setting in which we can speak freely is critical to the coaching process. Different people find different environments distracting. For some, the mere act of being in the office is a distraction. For others, public spaces such as cafes are rarely conducive to the candid conversations that empower the coaching process.

Sometimes, even our private offices or conference rooms are not ideal. A knock at the door, the sound of conversations going on around us, or inadvertently making eye contact with someone through a glass wall can take our attention away at critical moments in the conversation. Such seemingly insignificant events can trigger concern about speaking freely or send our minds spinning off on unrelated or irrelevant tangents.

Donna's building affords little privacy. There are few walls, fewer doors, and conference rooms with floor-to-ceiling windows. During her initial coaching session, Donna realized that she felt awkward meeting with her coach in a fishbowl conference room. She found herself wondering what her colleagues would ask about her meeting, and she was careful not to express her emotions for fear of being seen by those walking by. As a result of noticing her own discomfort, Donna started teleworking on the days she had calls with her coach. She made sure that her house would be empty on these days, too. She rescheduled calls on the days that her kids were home from school or her husband home from work. In addition to feeling more at ease, Donna discovered that she was more capable of gaining perspective on workplace challenges, and could more easily see how her style of managing her organization mirrored her style of managing her relationships with her kids, spouse, and even extended family.

We do ourselves (and our coaches) a huge favor when we proactively safeguard against anything that might take our attention away from the coaching conversation. When we eliminate both internal and external distractions, we can protect the mental space necessary to participate fully in dialogue with our coach.

Application

Identify one or more places in which will you feel free to engage with your coach fully and without reservation. Here's a test: Go to the space where you're being coached. Think of the scariest truth that you could say out loud— something that nearly no one knows. Can you say it out loud, without whispering, in that space? Imagine yourself getting very upset in a conversation. Can you imagine yourself breaking down without worrying about others' noticing? If you want to get the most out of your coaching conversations, you will need to find or create space in which you can speak and act freely. If you cannot think of a safe place for your coaching meetings, ask your coach for recommendations.

Create a short checklist of ways that you will eliminate environmental distractions during your coaching sessions. Block off five to ten minutes prior to your coaching session to allow time for you to go through the items on your checklist. Checklist items may include:

- Place a "do not disturb" sign on your office door.
- Let key people know that you'll be unavailable for an hour and give them a special way to reach you only in case of emergency.
- Set your phone to silent, and/or lock it in an office drawer.
- Get something to eat and drink.
- Use the restroom.
- Have tissues handy.
- Shut down your computer or move away from it.

Notes

Tip 21. Focus on Yourself

"Why compare yourself with others? No one in the entire world can do a better job of being you than you."
– Unknown

The coaching process is personal; it is about who we are and what we can change in ourselves. While we may aspire to have a certain effect on others (e.g., to motivate them or to improve their performance), we can't change other people. We must focus on ourselves. As we explore our own personality, preferences, tendencies, strengths, and challenges, we may need to balance the inclination to compare ourselves with others by reminding ourselves of how much progress we have made.

We are all prone to thinking that our developmental benchmarks are outside of us—that they are in the people we look up to, the labels placed upon us, or in our social status. Some evolutionary biologists argue we are even genetically programmed to compare ourselves to others. The problem is these comparisons often come with significant downsides, including guilt, shame, and decreased happiness. All of these effects are enemies of learning. However, using our own development path as the grounds for comparison supports a healthier mindset—one that promotes growth and fulfillment.

The key to maintaining an inward focus lies with our own power of self-observation. When we are keen self-observers, we notice how we see things and how our perception changes over time. We could, for example, compare what we know now to what we knew then, our current personal standards to our former standards, our current behavior to our past behavior, or our current beliefs to our old beliefs.

Paul needed his senior team members to start acting more like leaders. He needed them to think strategically and to communicate a shared message to junior team members. Paul entered into his coaching engagement hoping to learn strategies for molding his senior staff into leaders. Only when Paul fully relinquished his agenda of "bringing them along" did he realize that his own perspective was getting in the way of their growth.

With time, Paul began to focus on his own perspective toward his team members. He noticed shifts in the way he saw each one of them. He noticed when his mind was more and less open to a new way of viewing someone. He began to realize how much his self-awareness had increased. One day, Paul reflected on his growth in comparison to the growth of his team members. Once again, he found himself in the judge's seat. This time, however, Paul quickly realized that his mind had wandered into territory that didn't serve him well, and he quickly redirected his thoughts back to his own development goals.

Application

For the duration of your coaching engagement, eliminate as many triggers of self-comparison from your life as possible. Consider, for example, the various media sources (magazines, television, Facebook, etc.) that you access on a regular basis. Avoid messages that tell you that you need to be a certain way. Take a break from people who make you feel inferior or who encourage you to think you should be anything other than yourself.

Search the Internet for a picture of "people talking." Any scene of people talking to one another will do. On a sheet of paper, write down what you think is happening in the scene. Then imagine that you are in this scene. What do you do next? Next, share the same image with three friends or colleagues. Without divulging your own responses, ask your friends or colleagues to respond to the same two questions ("What is going on here?" and, "If you were in this scene, what would you do next?"). Get together to share your responses. Discuss these questions:

- In what ways did we each see the situation differently?
- How did our perceptions affect our choices of what to do next?
- Which actions could be available to us if we saw the situation differently?
- What does our individual perception of the situation say about each of us?

Notes

Tip 22. Start With an Accomplishment

"Much of the stress that people feel doesn't come from having too much to do. It comes from not finishing what they started."
– David Allen

One of the ways to handle the added responsibilities the coaching engagement offers us is to start each day with a small accomplishment. Research suggests, and experience often proves, that accomplishment breeds accomplishment. If we start our day by getting something done, we are more likely to get a lot done. Our coaching conversations and assignments can either be weights that drag our to-do list to new depths of impossibility, or opportunities to get rolling on personal development.

Admiral William McRaven shared the following story at his commencement address to the University of Texas: "Every morning in basic SEAL training, my instructors, who at the time were all Vietnam veterans, would show up in my barracks room, and the first thing they would inspect was [my] bed. If you did it right, the corners would be square, the covers pulled tight, the pillow centered just under the headboard, and the extra blanket folded neatly at the foot of the rack—rack—that's Navy talk for bed. It was a simple task—mundane at best. But every morning we were required to make our bed to perfection. It seemed a little ridiculous at the time, particularly in light of the fact that we were aspiring to be real warriors, tough battle-hardened SEALs—but the wisdom of this simple act has been proven to me many times over. If you make your bed every morning, you will have accomplished the first task of the day. It will give you a small sense of pride, and it will encourage you to do another task, and another and another."

Application

Create a list of seven tasks that you desperately want to get done this week. They don't have to be time-intensive, but they do need to be important to you. Perhaps there's a card you've been meaning to send, a squeaky door that is annoying you every time you open it, or a cluttered desk that would be beautiful if cleared off. Complete one task per day, first thing in the morning, for seven days. Observe the impact this has on your week.

Notes

Awareness

Tip 23. Center Yourself

"At the center of your being
you have the answer;
you know who you are
and you know what you want."
— Lao Tzu, philosopher

To varying extents, we go through life being pulled around by thoughts and feelings, chasing after ambiguous and moving targets, and rarely reflecting on the extent to which we are hitting any mark at all. We spend most of our time reacting to the world around us, coping with life rather than creating an internal environment that supports the life we want to lead. Coaching is an opportunity to switch from a reactive stance to a creative stance, and we enable this switch by getting centered.

"Centered" describes a state in which we are present to our body and intentional regarding our thoughts and feelings. When we are centered, we stop the frenetic motion of our bodies and our minds. We become grounded by the reality of where we are and what is available to us in that very moment alone. From this place emerges the capacity to clarify what we want and to honestly assess how far we have to go. Centering is especially important when we feel pushed or pulled by what is going on around and inside of us.

Charles, the leader of an international design team, often showed up for coaching sessions visibly off balance. He rocked back and forth in his chair, his eyes darted around the room, and his fingers fidgeted with the papers in front of him. Charles felt himself pulled in all directions, at all times of the day and night. He found it difficult to focus on conversations, both with his coach and with his team.

Charles' coach challenged him to adopt a centering practice. At first Charles struggled—he found sitting still in his chair awkward and unnatural. His coach encouraged him to identify a position of strength and stability that was familiar to him. As an avid cyclist, Charles realized that he was most stable when "in the drops," perched over the drop bars of his bike, weight in his legs, and feet balanced on the pedals. Charles recognized that he could quickly center himself by recreating this position at this desk. With one foot planted in front of the other, sitting on the edge of his seat with his forearms resting on the desk in front of him, Charles felt as stable as in the saddle of his bicycle.

Application

Make it a practice to start your day by going through this centering exercise: Sit in your office chair or in another upright chair. Place both feet on the ground, feeling both the balls of your feet and your heels in contact with the ground. Take your hands and place them on your thighs. Close your eyes and expand your body along all three dimensions. On the vertical plane, feel your spine lengthen. On the horizontal plane, allow your shoulders to stretch away from your body, to expand toward the sides of the chair. Finally, explore the depth of your body in the chair. Invite your chest to fill with air, and allow your belly to expand outward with a deep breath. How much room can you take up in each direction? Once you have explored these limits, bring your focus back to your feet. Feel their connection to the ground. Visualize your feet absorbing energy from the ground. Feel the energy rise up through each area of your body. Visualize the energy also flowing back into the ground. Visualize this flow of energy as vividly as you can—up from the ground, through each part of your body, and back into the ground—until you feel a sense of relaxation and deep connection to the ground. Say to yourself, "I am grounded." Finally, bring your focus to the center of your chest. Picture this as the center of your very being. Tell yourself, "I am centered."

Notes

Tip 24. Use Reminders to Break Patterns

Many of us lead such busy lives that we'd be lost without our calendars. We set reminders to attend meetings, make important calls, pick up the kids from school, remember deadlines, etc. Just as reminders can save us from forgetting these events, they can also be used to help us break habitual patterns of behaviors and/or adopt new ones.

Setting reminders to be intentional about behavioral patterns that support your coaching goals can ensure that these new patterns are not forgotten. If we are working on reducing our stress levels, for example, we might set a reminder to pause and take a couple of deep breaths before and after each meeting. If our goal is to increase self-confidence, we might set a reminder to stand tall and with confidence at the beginning of each hour, or to repeat an affirmation of our potential each morning. Reminders work best when they repeat at predictable and frequent intervals. An occasional or infrequent reminder is not nearly as powerful as one that reminds us at the top of each hour.

Since 2008, Joyce's phone has been programmed to chime at 2:00 p.m. with a message: "Breathe." It reminds her to close her eyes in the middle of the day, even for a few seconds, and center herself. Building this simple practice into her day has helped Joyce to integrate relaxation into her life wherever she is—while working, in a meeting, in transit. Joyce even gets her kids to take a few deep breaths with her when they're together.

Interval timers, which are specifically designed to notify us at pre-determined intervals throughout the day, can be particularly useful, as they can be set to offer reminders in an unobtrusive way, such as by vibrating or playing a short tone. They can be purchased as individual devices; some are supported by certain wristwatches, and a number exist as free apps for smartphones.

Application

Identify one new behavior in support of a coaching goal that you seek to engage in consistently. Determine the ideal frequency of this new behavior; be willing to stretch a little beyond what you're initially comfortable with. Set a reminder that will consistently remind you to engage in this new behavior at this specific interval.

Notes

Tip 25. Keep a Development Log

"The faintest ink is more powerful than the strongest memory."
– Chinese proverb

When we're in the midst of personal transformation, we need all the support we can get. There will be times when we wonder if coaching is working for us. We may feel drained and uncertain of whether the ambiguity and discomfort of the coaching process is worth the promise of transformation. Even with a strong support community, we may find ourselves lacking the motivation to push on. Acknowledgement can go a long way in reenergizing us. But rather than looking to and waiting for others to acknowledge our growth, we can acknowledge it ourselves. When we need acknowledgement, we can give ourselves that very gift.

Jane kept a running list of the various ways that she saw herself growing, and the impact(s) associated with that growth on her personal life. As she put it, "By catching myself acting as if assumptions are fact, and then questioning those assumptions, my husband and I have had fewer misunderstandings. And by realizing almost immediately when I'm getting upset, I can consistently ward off an angry outburst and even a snide remark by acknowledging the feeling and letting it pass."

Application

At the end of each day, take a moment and thank yourself for the efforts you have made to improve your life, no matter how small. If possible, do this aloud, mentioning each accomplishment one at a time and pausing between each to feel the endorphins that result from doing this. For added benefit, you can do this while looking at yourself in the mirror. Speak to yourself as you would a friend whom you would like to encourage. Here are some examples of language you can use to get started. Be sure to modify the language to best fit your personality.

- "I want to take a moment to acknowledge myself for _____. Although it may seem small, this action represents movement in a positive direction. Thank you for taking this step."

- "I am proud of myself for doing _____ today. It will help me achieve my larger objectives by _____."

Notes

Tip 26. Remind Yourself With a Talisman

"To thine own self be true."
– Script on the back of Alcoholics Anonymous sobriety
anniversary medallions

A talisman is any object that is thought to have special qualities or bring good luck. In the context of coaching, a talisman is a personal item that prompts us to bring an idea or commitment to mind. A talisman can be something we wear (e.g., a ring or bracelet) or something we see (e.g., a photo, card, or banner across your office wall). Any object can be transformed into a talisman by the simple act of associating it in our minds with a clear and concise idea or intention. That object then holds a very specific meaning to us.

As helpful as a talisman can be in helping us re-orient our thoughts and stay true to our commitments, the greatest evidence of a talisman's impact lies in the moment when it is no longer useful to us. Our hope is that a talisman will prompt inner transformation that then renders the talisman itself unnecessary.

Shortly after the events of September 11, 2001, Daniel developed a fear of flying. At the time, his consulting roles required travel both domestically and internationally for at least a week per month. The nights before each flight were sleepless and each travel experience stressful. Daniel's neighbor sensed his stress and gave him a small coin with an angel imprinted on one side. She promised it would keep him safe. Daniel was touched by his neighbor's kindness and carried it with him. Each time he felt the coin in his pocket, he was reminded of her kindness. He did not even need to look at the coin—merely putting his hand in his pocket and feeling it there brought him a sense of calm. After a few months, Daniel's fear of flying subsided, and he was able to travel without it.

Cary integrated a talisman into her phone by setting her background to a picture of her family. Merely looking at it reminded her, "Family first!" It represented her commitment to be home to her son by 4:30 p.m. each day. This specific association ensured that this talisman had a powerful impact. Without such a clear association with a specific idea, the picture would still remind her of her family, but it would lack the ability to impact her behavior and decision to truly put family first.

Application

Identify one thought or commitment that would transform your life. Find an item that can remind you of this transformational concept. Create a specific association for that item, and declare it to be a reminder to you of that association. Keep it nearby; carry it with you, if possible.

Notes

Priority

Tip 27. Clarify Expectations

A coach can serve many functions within the overarching purpose of helping us accomplish our growth and development goals. As we get accustomed to our coach's style and approach, it helps to clarify what we want our coach to provide, and to what degree. To what extent would we like him or her to challenge us? To what extent would we like our coach to help us think through a problem before offering advice? How much support do we expect our coach to provide? If we do not reflect on these questions and communicate our expectations to our coach, we may find ourselves frustrated with the experience. We might become more resistant to our coach's suggestions, or may even disengage entirely. And yet so often, a simple and direct request made of our coach can get us back on track.

Identifying our expectations and communicating them to our coach also opens the door to a critical question: What if our expectations for coaching fall short of helping us accomplish our goals? For example, what if we expect our coach to provide advice when we really need to be challenged to come up with a unique idea of our own? A conversation about any gaps between our expectations and what a coach offers to us can turn a disappointment into a breakthrough.

Lee, an associate director, was referred to a coach by his CEO. The CEO was concerned that Lee's direct approach upset members of senior management. Lee agreed that his relationship with senior managers was confrontational and set a goal to improve his interactions with them. Lee's coach laid out what Lee could expect from her: to ask questions that Lee didn't know how to answer, to listen beyond the words Lee spoke, to present observations for his consideration, to challenge his understanding of situations and of people, and to hold him accountable to commitments he made.

Halfway through the coaching engagement, Lee realized that he also expected his coach to be a sounding board for his frustrations with senior management and to support his viewpoint when the coach interacted with management in other capacities. Lee brought these expectations to his coach, and they discussed what the coach could do to support Lee's need to manage frustrations and to have his voice heard by his management.

Application

Share your expectations with your coach and ask what you can expect from him or her. Consider your specific objectives for the coaching engagement, your expected timeframe for the achievement of those objectives, and what level of dedication to the process you will commit.

Notes

Tip 28. Protect Your Coaching

The space we dedicate to coaching will need to be protected from time to time. Protecting our coaching might involve setting boundaries and expectations among clients, colleagues, family, and friends; tidying up loose ends on projects; arranging for support services (e.g., a babysitter); or asking someone else to cover our responsibilities on a project. Often, keeping our plate clear requires that we develop the ability to say "no" to new commitments. For many of us, this is not as easy as it sounds.

In the days or weeks prior to beginning the coaching engagement, it is important to consider the different ways we might respond to requests for our time. Many of us find it difficult to turn down opportunity, and it may be necessary for us to think about how we can make this easier. If you're the type of person who frequently finds yourself overcommitted, this will be especially important.

William, a transportation-planning executive, had grown accustomed to rescheduling appointments. When he began preparing for his first coaching engagement, he decided to do what he could to set expectations that there would be times when he would be unavailable, as he was dedicated to getting the most he could out of the process. Lacking a way to express this, he worked with his coach to develop a short script he could use to ensure that the time he would dedicate to coaching would be protected:

"Just so you know, _____, I'm going to be busier than usual in the coming months. I'm going to be working with a coach to develop my leadership skills. We will be meeting on Thursday afternoons from 4:00 to 5:30 for the next twelve weeks. This time is important to me. I'd like your help running defense on any meetings or responsibilities that could impact my ability to make these appointments."

Application

Reflect and/or journal on the following questions:

- What conflicts might impact your ability to fully engage in the coaching process? How will you handle these conflicts?
- What can you do today to set expectations for your availability among your clients, colleagues, and even friends and family?
- What requests might you make of others to ensure the space you dedicate to your development is protected?

Notes

Tip 29. Schedule for Stability

"Things that matter most must never be at the mercy of things which matter least."
– Goethe

We all have elements in our lives that are unreliable and unpredictable; we all face the friction of day-to-day activities. For many of us, coaching can feel like "one more thing" we have to plan for and fit into an already long list of responsibilities. We can ease this feeling by strategically choosing a day and time for our coaching sessions—one that is least likely to be interrupted by unplanned meetings and events. In this way, our session can serve as an anchor to our otherwise hectic schedules.

As the assistant director of a large government agency, Eleanor's schedule was unpredictable. She often found herself putting out fires and was constantly forced to adapt to shifting priorities. She had become notorious for being late to appointments and appearing distracted, as she would attempt to multitask during meetings.

When she first started working with her coach, he challenged her to find a way to anchor her week with something predictable, as a way of gaining a measure of control over her hectic schedule. Finding this notion difficult, he suggested that she try using the coaching sessions, as they represented something she had complete control over and could schedule in advance.

Eleanor and her coach proceeded to schedule every session of the coaching engagement. By blocking out that time on her schedule in advance, she created a predictable component of her week that would help her focus and prioritize her responsibilities. This, in turn, helped her to develop a more balanced and strategic approach to managing her professional roles. Eleanor soon found other small ways to add stability to her schedule, and before long approached her professional role in a more relaxed and influential manner.

Set your coaching engagement on a foundation of reliability and predictability so that it can support you through the unexpected and the undesirable. See if you can find a regular interval between coaching meetings—a frequency that is sustainable and that maintains momentum by regularly pushing you into action.

Application
Reflect and/or journal on the following questions:
- When in the week do you find yourself most desiring space to pause?
- How can the sessions of your coaching engagement be scheduled so that they offer you something predictable, and even something that you can look forward to?

Notes

Tip 30. Blame it on Coaching

"The ~~dog~~ coach made me do it."
– Carylynn

In our attempt to evolve personally and professionally, it is always best to begin from a place of honesty. To the best of our ability, we must own the whole process. We can facilitate this by sharing our development goals with others and being open about the changes that we're trying to make in ourselves and in our behavior. There are times, however, when we will want to make a change without fully explaining ourselves. Sometimes the situation or timing isn't right. Sometimes we don't feel comfortable sharing our development goals with a certain person or group of people. In these cases, rather than drastically shifting our behavior without any explanation at all, we can simply point to our coaching process itself as the reason for change.

Tony was overwhelmed by all the projects and activities to which he had committed. Overwork and overwhelm were patterns for Tony. Through coaching, Tony realized the impact that these patterns had on himself, his relationships, and his results. Tony committed to saying "no" to new work projects until he finished up a few of the ones on his plate.

When Tony's mother-in-law asked him to help her paint her house, Tony did not feel that it was appropriate to explain the competing commitments on his plate, nor did he want to discuss his personal development goal. Instead, Tony simply said, "I'm working with a coach, and he asked me to commit to saying 'no' to new responsibilities until I clear up the loose ends on projects I have already started." Tony's mother-in-law was surprised, as Tony had never turned down one of her requests. Nonetheless, she had no reason to be offended and respected the commitment he made to his coach.

Application

Reflect on the changes you are making in your behavior as a result of coaching. Consider how others are responding to these changes. Are there people who might be more understanding and supportive of these changes if they were better aware of the reasoning behind them? If so, talk to your coach about what explanations you might offer, to help others understand and be more supportive of the changes you make.

Notes

Section Three:
The Growth Mindset

Perspective

Tip 31. Embrace 'Beginnerhood'

"Lose your cleverness and pick up bewilderment."
– Rumi

Our sense of knowing may be our biggest barrier to growth. When we (Daniel & Cary) began our coach training program, we were asked to write the following note in our journals: "I am a great coach. And in the domain of coaching, I am a beginner." For many of us, neither statement rang true. It felt audacious to claim greatness as a coach in the presence of truly masterful coaches serving as faculty. It felt similarly inauthentic to claim beginnerhood in a domain in which we had many years of experience. For some of us, it felt odd that these two statements could co-exist. How could we be great coaches and beginners? Weren't the great coaches the ones who had it all figured out?

Since that time, we have learned that there is nothing further from the truth. Our greatness is made possible by declaring ourselves beginners, regardless (and in spite) of our past experiences, expertise, and beliefs.

Don began working with a coach when he realized that he did not want to become a part of his current company's senior leadership team. Don felt disconnected with the company's values and wanted to explore opportunities outside the company.

Don entered the coaching relationship "knowing" that his career path was somewhere within his current industry. He had worked in the industry for thirty years. Don didn't see any future for himself outside it—not for lack of interest but simply because he "knew" that no other company would be interested in him. Don's coach challenged him to reflect on how well this assumption served him. Don agreed to question his belief, and in doing so, he realized that his leadership skills were transferable to positions in many sectors. Don discovered many unexpected opportunities, and he realized that these opportunities only presented themselves after he declared himself a beginner in the domain of his own job search.

Application

Notice your use of absolute language (e.g., "That will never work"). Practice transforming absolute statements into less absolute terms, for example, by beginning the statements with the phrase, "It seems..." (e.g., "It seems that will never work").

Notes

Tip 32. Cultivate Curiosity

"Could you allow it to be other than you think it is?"
– Larry Crane

Curiosity may be the single most important quality to adopt throughout your coaching engagement. Curiosity is the antidote to getting stuck in our assumptions and beliefs, which can be tremendous barriers to personal growth. We're far more likely to try our hand at something if we wonder whether we can do it, rather than believe that we can or can't do it. Curiosity keeps our brains engaged in interesting questions and prevents us from jumping to conclusions. Even from within the most challenging life conditions, the possibility of something new and different is always present—we just have to be curious enough to look for it. Curiosity creates new possibilities for us.

Curiosity is just like a muscle. It can atrophy when not used, and will grow stronger the more it is exercised and engaged in new and different ways. Even gentle workouts, like asking a follow-up question, can build this muscle. It is never too early or too late to begin exercising our curiosity muscle.

Lin and his coach were exploring why he gets irritated when peers question him on (seemingly) simple and obvious decisions. A strong thinker, Lin was full of judgments about himself and his peers. "It's ridiculous for me to get worked up over this. Bob has no idea what's going on. Sue likes to challenge me on everything." When Lin reflected on these assumptions, he realized that they only held him back from learning more about himself and his colleagues.

As part of a coaching assignment, Lin started practicing curiosity. In every conversation, Lin played Curious George. He probed, he asked, he explored, and he did so playfully and with as much genuine interest as he could muster. As a result, he learned all sorts of things about his peers, and their relationship improved dramatically—something that Lin never before believed was in the realm of possibility.

Application

For one week, have at least one conversation per day in which you practice extreme curiosity. As you listen to others, think of at least one follow-up question you might ask, even if you think you know what the answer might be. Alternatively, if you catch yourself adhering too rigidly to an assumption, think of a way to challenge that assumption. Leverage curiosity to probe into it.

Notes

Tip 33. Learn From Dead Ends

"When your coach gives you lemons, make lemonade."
— Daniel

The coaching process requires a willingness to explore. Just as in a maze, occasionally, we'll walk down one path only to find that a better path had been just a few steps behind the one we chose. From time to time, coaches ask questions that do not feel relevant. In fact, sometimes they are not. Quite often, breakthrough moments come as the direct result of questions that are indirectly related to the conversation, or that even demand we change the course of the conversation entirely.

If we view the moments that feel like dead ends as a waste of time, they are certain to be just that. If we stay open to the possibility that they are part and parcel of the larger process of self-inquiry, we realize that there are no dead ends at all, unless we perceive them as such. They are, in fact, a necessary part of the adventure.

Application
Reflect and/or journal on the following questions:
- Could you allow for the possibility that this feeling of being stuck is just a feeling and not necessarily a reality?

- How is this apparent dead end an opportunity for action or new ways of thinking?
- How does what you have learned from running into this dead end empower you?

Notes

Tip 34. Treat Inquiry as Action

"Coaching is balcony time."
– Scott Eblin

Scott Eblin, a highly accomplished coach and author, has suggested that transformation requires time on the dance floor (action) and time on the balcony (self-observation). Most people work with a coach, at least in part, to identify and overcome barriers to success. To the extent that this is true for us, self-inquiry is a critical part of the process. Most of us have a difficult time diving into self-inquiry. After dipping our toes in with a simple reflection activity or two, we chase after a plan for improving ourselves, our teams, and/or our organization.

Time spent in self-reflection can feel like a waste, especially for hard-charging success-minded types. We're so used to "doing" that the mere thought of thinking about what we're doing and how we're doing it seems unproductive. It can feel like an indulgence to "know thyself," and knowing thyself more doesn't necessarily feel like making progress. But if you want to approach your life intentionally, self-inquiry is absolutely necessary. Self-inquiry clarifies our objectives and purpose. It reveals opportunities for course correction. Self-inquiry *is* action.

Application

For one week, challenge yourself to validate self-inquiry as an activity that is as worthy of your time as eating or sleeping. See if you can incorporate at least a few minutes of self-reflection into every day. Schedule some time between meetings and events to simply consider how things are going: Which behaviors are serving you and should be continued? Which behaviors are not serving you and should be abandoned? Which behaviors require just a bit of refinement to move more powerfully toward your objectives?

Notes

Integration

Tip 35. Allow Spillover

As leadership coaches, we are often asked how our work differs from that of career and life coaches. These forms of coaching are distinguishable in terms of their primary and initial objectives, but to compartmentalize them is to suggest that our leadership is disconnected from our career and/or our life. Part of the power in a coaching engagement is to investigate and unravel the degree to which our behaviors are influenced by situational context. At one extreme, we can think that our behaviors are 100 percent dependent on the situation. At the other extreme, we can think that we are who we are, regardless of our situation.

The reality is that we exhibit situation-specific tendencies, as well as more global tendencies, all the time. For example, we may extend trust easily in personal and professional relationships alike, while only certain situations trigger us to be assertive. Through coaching, we begin to recognize which of our behavioral tendencies follow us everywhere.

We're likely to realize that these "all the time" behaviors deserve at least as much attention as those that are specific to any given situation.

We can maximize the value we gain from our coach by allowing our growth in one domain to spill over into others. The insights we gain while developing ourselves professionally through coaching will be relevant to other areas of our life. In fact, those insights will ultimately be as valuable as they are applicable to various areas of our life. As we achieve our coaching objectives, we can look at the areas of our life to see if the same patterns are at play, and learn to apply the same achievement strategies in these other domains. We maximize our return on investment when we allow the benefits of the coaching process to transcend our immediate objectives.

Colin is an extrovert and enjoys a healthy social life. He is easy to talk to, and people have a tendency to open up to him, both at work and in his personal life. Through working with a leadership coach, Colin recognized that his willingness to share his vulnerabilities satisfied a need for approval but sacrificed the ability to be taken seriously. As Colin learned to be more judiciously vulnerable, his relationships with colleagues and fellow managers improved.

While Colin first thought that the shift in his behavior was only necessary at work, he soon realized that the same dynamic was at play in his personal life, and that he could build stronger relationships in his personal life by applying a similar discretion. By allowing an insight gained through leadership coaching to spill over into his personal life, Colin found that a small change in his behavior equally improved the nature of both his professional and personal relationships, and he discovered a way to make the value of the coaching experience transcend his professional objectives.

Application

Identify one discovery you have made about yourself through the coaching process. Consider how this insight may be applied in both your professional life and in your personal life. Share these reflections with your coach.

Notes

Tip 36. Fit Coaching Into Your Plan

Whether the specific objective of coaching was set by us or by our employer, it does not exist in a vacuum. The context for this objective should always be our longer-term development plan. We can start by determining how the coaching objective fits into our larger professional objective. At the outset of each coaching session, we can then create a goal for that conversation that supports our larger coaching objectives. Each smaller goal serves the achievement of the larger ones.

Adam, a coach, has a great way to approach the nesting of shorter and longer-term goals for himself He starts his personal goal-setting process by setting a long-term vision, at least ten years out. He then works backward, asking himself the question, "What actions do I need to take to accomplish this goal?" The answers to this question generate shorter-term goals, in the three- to five-year range. Asking the question again generates his nine- to twelve-month goals. Finally, he is able to take this process to the smallest scale, which might be a goal for a single coaching session or a shorter-term learning path.

It is likely that we will find ambiguity in at least one of these time frames. We may have only loosely defined professional objectives; we may not know exactly what we can expect from a coaching engagement; and we may have a hard time defining what we want to get out of any given session. There is, however, magic in this process, as it reveals the relationships between near-term actions and long-term results.

Application

Have a conversation with your coach or a close confidant about how the specific objectives you have set for coaching support the achievement of your longer-term goals. If you have a hard time articulating the connection, be willing to consider revising your coaching goals.

Ask your coach for permission to stay in touch after the coaching engagement ends. Once or twice a year, reach out to your coach and let him or her know what you've been doing differently as of late. Share any insights you've had. Let your former coach also know what's not working so well for you.

Notes

Tip 37. Leverage Assessments

Assessments come in many forms, including skill and ability tests, personality and preference inventories, performance reviews, customer feedback surveys, and measures of physical health. The results of assessments can help us gain deeper insight into many aspects of our lives. Assessment results are not intended to put us in a box from which we can never escape. Nor should they be cast away as meaningless. Assessment results are simply data points.

When the numbers in our assessment results don't match our expectations, we may be tempted to spend more time critiquing the measure than inquiring about what it means to us. However, when we're open to the complexity of these seemingly contradictory data points, we often achieve breakthroughs in self-awareness. The key to obtaining significant value from assessments is to look for threads of truth running through the data, which include both the assessment results and the interpretations of our own experience. When we treat assessment data as something worth exploring, we will likely find threads that lead us to areas for growth.

Lisa was deeply disturbed by her leadership assessment report. "Have you ever seen anyone with scores so bad?" she asked her coach. "Should I just quit?" Lisa's coach encouraged her to put the assessment in context. She was new to the organization. Her team said they loved her.

As Lisa explored the patterns in the data, such as an indicator that she was too passive in senior management meetings, her eyes opened to a new possibility. Could it be that her scores reflected the potential that people saw in her? Lisa explored a new story: Her people believed in her; they saw how much she was capable of, and it pained them to see her shrinking back from that potential. Lisa bravely shared an overview of her scores and her interpretation with a few trusted colleagues. They validated that while Lisa was falling short of their hopes, the data reflected high expectations for her and confidence in her ability to rise in leadership.

Application

Ask your coach to recommend one or more assessments and to review the results with you. Consider selecting assessments that reflect different aspects of being (e.g., personality, leadership, emotional intelligence, conflict management style). Be willing to discuss both the results that confirm your beliefs about yourself and those that do not.

Notes

Tip 38. Use Language Strategically

"Change your language, change yourself."
— Chalmers Brothers

The words we use have the power to broaden the way we think and even to expand the options available to us. Each time we say "yes," we create a different reality for ourselves; the same is true each time we say "no." In the domain of personal transformation, our language impacts the reality of who we can become.

Even more notable than our choice of words, the tense we choose is the key to using language for transformation. In the past tense, we can speak to the qualities that we want to leave behind. In the present tense, we can speak to the qualities that we want to embody. Choice of tense is more than a semantic trick. Choosing the tense that reflects where we want to be teaches our mind to see unwanted perspectives or patterns of behavior as coming to an end, and suggests to us the possibility that we can adopt new perspectives and cultivate new ways of being.

Joe is a popular team leader who likes to get along and avoid conflict at all costs. At the beginning of his coaching engagement, Joe described himself in a way that reaffirmed his identity as conflict-avoidant: "I don't like conflict. Sometimes, however, I need to be able to say the hard truths." In time, Joe changed his language in order to put his avoidant self in the past: "The many times that I avoided conflict in my life taught me it is not worth the tradeoff." Putting his self-defeating identify in the past opened the door for Joe to claim a new reality: "When I choose to step into difficult conversations, I'm a fantastic mediator."

Application

Identify one shift you would like to make in yourself. Begin using the past tense to describe your current state, and begin using the present tense to describe your future state.

Notes

Tip 39. Learn to Improvise

Coaching can push us into new territory. What we do when we're on new ground will determine what we gain from the experience. One approach to dealing with the unexpected is to apply lessons from our past. For example, we can repeat something we've said in the past or repeat a process that has worked for us before. This approach is akin to recycling our experiences; it shows us new uses for capacities that we already possess. Recycling leads to learning, but in a somewhat limited way. Personal transformation may require the emergence of completely new capacities.

An alternative approach to navigating new terrain—one that fosters creativity and innovation—is to improvise. Children serve as excellent role models in this way; they improvise constantly. No shovel? Use a stick. No sword? A slightly longer stick is perfect. No horse? A branch is all we need to gallop across the field. Many of us find that improvising feels risky and even foolish. In our coaching work, we find that our clients' natural capacity to improvise is often undermined by overreliance on protocols and scripts. In other words, it's not a matter of learning to improvise so much as a matter of stopping ourselves from relying on our default way of being.

Music instructors understand how to balance knowledge and theory with improvisation and serendipity. Improvising in the domain of music means setting aside scales and standards, and playing freely. A common approach is to ask students to spend half of their time studying theory and the other half of their time playing anything they like, continuously and without stopping. This balance maximizes adherence to tradition, while inspiring creativity and, somewhat paradoxically, imbuing a sense of respect for tradition. As students develop, they find a healthy balance between honoring time-tested practice regimens and finding their own voice on the instrument.

This approach also inspires students to set aside self-judgment. The improvising musician will keep playing when he hits a dissonant note, rather than stopping dead in his tracks. In doing so, the self-critical voice within grows quieter and quieter.

Application

Identify a project or initiative that you are working on that will allow room for a creative solution. Try using a stream-of-consciousness method, either by writing or speaking, to discover new answers and approaches. If writing, begin simply writing words at random, and see what comes up. If speaking aloud, begin by making sounds and allowing whatever words come to mind to come out, even if they seem like nonsense. Do this for five minutes without stopping, then ask yourself: What new idea, product, or solution does this inspire?

Notes

Acknowledgement

Tip 40. Give Yourself Credit

There are times when our coach will do or say something that cascades into a breakthrough moment for us. A coach's observation can change our way of looking at ourselves. A coach's question can lead us to reframe our life. A coach's challenge can trigger a new career trajectory. At such times, it's tempting to give our coach the credit for these transformations. In truth, only we can bring about transformation for ourselves.

In order to gain the most from our coaching engagement, we need to give ourselves credit for our growth. A coach's observation will only change our way of looking at ourselves when we are ready to look at ourselves differently. A coach's question can only have an impact when we're open to considering it. A coach's challenge can only change our trajectory when we are ready to change. Many things may happen during the coaching engagement, but only because the whole of our life prepared us for it.

It can be easy to ignore the events that precipitate breakthrough moments. It's important for us to acknowledge the work that we've put into the process of self-inquiry and self-development that leads up to "tipping point" events, as it is only through recognizing and acknowledging the work that we've put in—the work that led up to these moments—that we can fully appreciate both the journey and the prizes along the way.

Myra had sought a coach when she transitioned from academia to a competitive international corporation. Her first months were painfully difficult, and for a time she felt that her coach was the only person with whom she could talk openly. Within a year, Myra learned how to navigate the company's politics, built strong relationships and a profitable new business line, and was promoted.

As her coaching engagement came to a close, Myra told her coach that she "never could have made it" without her. "Do you really think that's true?" her coach asked. "If it weren't for me, would you not have figured out another way? And if that's true, then don't you deserve the credit for your own growth?" Myra laughed and agreed.

Application

Make a list of key decisions you made and/or actions you took that resulted in personal growth. Put this list in a place where you can find it when you need a reminder that you deserve the credit for your own transformation.

Notes

Tip 41. Make a Personal Investment

"For where your treasure is, there your heart will be also."
– Matthew 21:6 (Holy Bible, New International Version)

Generally speaking, we put much more time, energy, and care into the items and activities that we pay for personally than those that are provided to us. We are more likely to attend a show or a convention that we purchase tickets for than one that is free to the public. We are more likely to read a book that we pay for than one that is given to us. There is a powerful psychological mechanism at play here. When we pay for something out of pocket, we gain a deeper sense of ownership over it.

This same mechanism applies to personal development. When we pay for our college tuition, we take our studies more seriously. When we pay for a training course, we listen more intently. When we invest personally in our coaching engagement, we are more likely to stay committed to our goals and to the coaching process. The personal investment we make in coaching automatically sends our minds on a subconscious search for returns.

Application

If the cost of coaching is coming out of your own pocket, reflect on the value of this personal investment by considering the alternative uses of your money. If your organization is paying for your coaching engagement, find a way to invest personally.

- Schedule sessions on your own time rather than on the corporate clock.
- Make an unplanned donation to a cause; match the amount of your donation to the personal financial value of accomplishing your coaching objectives.
- Pay for someone who does not have the financial resources for coaching (e.g., the head of a local non-profit, an emerging leader in your community) to work with a coach.
- Buy your coach a cup of coffee . . . or go wild and buy him or her lunch.
- Treat yourself to a nice meal after your coaching sessions.

Notes

Tip 42. Distinguish Between Failure and Mistake

"A failure is not always a mistake—it may simply be the best one can do under the circumstances. The real mistake is to stop trying."
– B. F. Skinner

We allow maximum room for growth when we consider the distinction between failure and mistake. A mistake is an action that we take based on incorrect information or guidance. Failure is the absence of success. We often feel that our mistakes equate to failure, but this is rarely true. In fact, mistakes often lead to great accomplishments, and likewise, our greatest achievements are riddled with mistakes. When we realize the difference between a mistake and a failure, we can deal with these two experiences in vastly difference ways.

When we fail, we often need to dive into deep self-reflection to figure out how we can grow from the experience and what is next for us. We rarely need to respond to a mistake in the same manner. We may need to forgive ourselves, and at times we may need to request forgiveness from others. We may need to put a system in place to safeguard ourselves from making the same mistake in the future—but then we can look for the next win. In fact, because our brains remember mistakes more easily and more saliently than they remember wins, we need to actively search for wins. If we wait to acknowledge our success until we accomplish the holy grail of achievements, we lose momentum. This is particularly true when we are facing big challenges or changes.

Lisa, an audit lead for a financial firm, struggled with distracting thoughts about food and body consciousness. When work was particularly busy, food was ordered in for every meal and Lisa had difficulty focusing on her work. Lisa defined success as no longer being distracted by food, making healthy food choices, and accepting her body as it was. She viewed small improvements, such as having only a few snacks per day as opposed to snacking constantly throughout the day, as falling short of her goal. As a result, she felt like a failure every day until her belief in her ability to change dissolved.

When asked to begin viewing the smallest of accomplishments as wins, Lisa found that accomplishment breeds accomplishment. Congratulating herself for eating just a few snacks per day prompted her to make healthier meal choices. Making healthier choices prompted her to take a break from work and enjoy her food. Enjoying food prompted her to eat when she was hungry rather than stressed.

Application
Don't let your efforts go without proper acknowledgement. See if you can find the intention behind your efforts,

whether they manifested as successes or mistakes. Keep a list of all small wins and lessons learned that were associated with each of your coaching goals. Keep in mind that you can search for wins in your past as well as your present.

Make a list of the different ways in which you can acknowledge your accomplishments. Your list might include a special dinner out with a colleague or a friend, an afternoon off to simply relax, a massage, or a new tie.

Notes

Tip 43. Breathe Into Insights

In any given coaching session, we are likely to find at least one key takeaway. And between coaching sessions, we'll experience many more insights that build off these takeaways. The coaching process is designed to allow for the interplay between insights and the opportunity to act on them. As beautiful as the dance between insight and action can be, it is often rushed or interrupted. When we find an ideal rhythm between any given insight and our follow-up actions, we concurrently find instrumental growth.

Sometimes an insight is so powerful that it takes our breath away or knocks us off our feet. The emotional energy that arises can be strong, propelling us to leap into action. When an insight comes about with a lot of energy, we can simply breathe and welcome the energy for a moment. Developing the ability to welcome this rush of energy and to allow it to pass can help us to put our insights into proper context. Then, we can take action more consciously and without the added pressure of raw emotion. Our capacity for analytical thinking returns as the energy begins to subside, and we better see the potential of our new understanding and how to apply it. We might see an opportunity where we did not before, or perhaps understand how the insight might be useful for others.

Other times, there is a gap between an insight and an opportunity for action, and our insights fall through that gap. In order to stop the fast pace of everyday life from hijacking the full benefit of these insights, we must take proactive steps to capture insights before they fall away from us. We can bookmark insights by proactively creating ways to capture them at any moment. We can then return to our notes when we have the time and space to process them deeply.

David, a management consultant, shared, "As someone who has worked with a coach continuously for two years, I can tell you that the capacity for realization is one of the most addictive parts of the process. It's something I look forward to and have come to expect when working with great coaches. I have found through experience, however, that the emotional rush that accompanies these realizations can be very strong. There can be a tendency to want to stay engaged in the coaching process solely for these realizations, as opposed to translating the insights into practical applications."

Application

The next time you discover something about yourself that you didn't know before, close your eyes and take a few moments to simply breathe. Inhale. Exhale. Notice how the insight transforms in your mind, becoming more expansive and applicable. Notice how you can take action while bringing that calm and relaxed state with you, leaving behind any frenetic energy.

Imagine having an idea at this very moment that you do not want to lose. How will you make sure that it's recorded so that you can revisit it later?

Notes

Epilogue:
Applying These Principles
to Everyday Life

"Change can be easier than you think."
– Joe Griffin

The objective of this book was simple: to empower you with actionable guidance that helps you work smarter, not harder, to achieve breakthrough results both personally and professionally. For example, by beginning coaching engagements with clearly articulated goals, a willingness to look openly and honestly at any obstacles that may exist, and orchestrating a supportive environment, clients can "grease the wheels" on their personal and professional development initiatives. And while the tips in this book have been presented within the context of coaching, they are useful in any transformational endeavor. As obvious as this may seem, however, it is easy to lose sight of these ideas when we are knee-deep in our own growth process. Far beyond the context of coaching, this book serves as a useful and timely reminder of proven principles that make the change process easier. The tips you have read are applicable to any endeavor you might undertake to advance, learn, and grow. The themes covered by these tips –

initiative, community, momentum, self-care, focus, awareness, priority, perspective, integration, and acknowledgement – highlight your ultimate responsibility for your own development and well-being.

We hope that you will return to this book time and time again. Allow the tips herein to serve as reminders and tangible strategies for owning and taking responsibility for the intentions you set, the actions you take, and the results you experience. As you continually lean in to *Coaching Companion* concepts, you will begin to notice a deeper level of transformation –the increasing presence of a growth mindset. A growth mindset is one that supports continuous evolution by inviting the courage and will necessary to move forward boldly, even when the desired results are unclear or appear out of reach. As this mindset becomes more natural to you, you will increasingly view growth as a competency in itself. As a result, you will begin to see new opportunities to develop, hone, and leverage your own growth, in all areas of your life. Far beyond the duration and scope of your coaching engagements, *The Coaching Companion* will strengthen your growth "muscle" and empower you to achieve success beyond your wildest dreams.

Acknowledgements

Daniel and Cary would like extend their sincere gratitude to Junie Nathani for contributing such an excellent Foreword; to Pat Mathews, Chalmers Brothers, and Brandon Moreno for their glowing and humbling endorsements; to Estelle Kemp Parker, Brian Larson, Laura Forer and Katie Aberbach for their excellent reviewing and editing contributions; and to Lauren Weinstein for her advice on self-publishing. And above all, to a God whose grace and unconditional love fills us up so that we can serve this world.

Cary would also like to thank her mentor, John Keyser, whose insistence that she start writing after many years of complacency pulled her out of her rut; her husband, Ben, who told her to "go write" while he tackled the never-ending work of parenthood; and her son, Charlie Clay, whose energy and giggles made it impossible for the demands of writing a book to stand in the way of the most important things in life.

Daniel would also like to thank his wife, Tanya, for her endless love and support; his parents, Richard and Jo, for being as much friends as they are inspirations; Anabel Suarez, his longtime thought partner, coach, and friend, for her endless wisdom and uncanny ability to help him navigate the many challenges of life; and Alicia Rodriguez, whose mentoring and coaching inspired the courage to continue to uncover and honor his own unique voice.

About the Authors

Daniel Sheres

Daniel Sheres is a leadership coach based in Washington, DC. A former healthcare management consultant, he holds a Master's degree in Health Policy and Management and Certificate in Health Finance and Management from the Johns Hopkins University. He received his Certificate in Leadership Coaching from the Institute for Transformational Leadership at Georgetown University.

On a personal note

My own journey into coaching began as a client. I hired my first coach in 2007 to help me build my consulting business. Like many budding entrepreneurs, I had the skill to do the work, but didn't really understand how to win the work. I had a colleague who had worked with a coach and highly recommended it.

Before the first session, I remember expecting my coach to act a lot like a consultant. He would ask me questions about my services and strategy and then advise me on what to do. To my surprise, the first conversations weren't about the business at all, but about what motivated me. Initially, I played along, trusting the process as best I could. As we then began to get into the details of my professional objectives, I started to see the link between my inner motivators and goals, and the skills and behaviors I would need to develop to achieve those goals. Together we created a plan—and while I would be able to lean on my coach for support and guidance throughout the process, I knew that nothing would change without a sincere commitment from me.

I dedicated several hours each day to reading and practicing new behaviors. I learned how to market myself, negotiate deals, and set and achieve financial targets. I clarified my offer, honed my strengths, and identified the weaknesses that I would have to either develop or delegate. It was a transformative experience, to say the least; by the end of the six months I had nearly tripled my income, and had a backlog of work extending out almost a year. My fascination with the process of transformation quickly became a passion as I continued working with this coach for another year. Quite naturally, I found myself integrating coaching into my consulting roles, and six months later I began offering coaching as a service.

At the time of this writing, I have worked with a coach almost continuously for seven years and have been coaching professionally for five. Having been both a coach and a client has demonstrated to me the shared responsibility that exists in this unique partnership.

A qualified coach is only half the equation. The value a client receives from the coaching process is largely dependent on the client's willingness to fully engage in the process. As in many endeavors, it's not about working harder, but rather working smarter. It is my sincere hope that the advice presented in this book will help clients of all coaches realize the full value of their coaching engagement and achieve results well beyond what they initially thought possible.

Learn more about Daniel at www.danielsheres.com.

Carylynn Larson

Carylynn (Cary) Kemp Larson is a leadership coach based in the Washington, DC area, though her clients span the globe. Cary works with leaders across levels, from senior executives to team leads. She also works with those aspiring to leadership positions and seeking to make successful career transitions. Cary has coached in health and human services, pharmaceuticals, science and technology, manufacturing and engineering sectors. She has extensive experience working with scientists, engineers and entrepreneurs. Cary holds a Ph.D. in Organizational Psychology from George Mason University and a Certificate in Leadership Coaching from Georgetown University.

On a personal note

I have deep compassion for what my clients go through on the receiving end of the coaching engagement. It is hard to be coached. Coaching can be draining. For many of my clients as well as for me, this draining process is actually quite necessary. It is through the experience of being drained that we allow ourselves to be filled up with something new, something more than the muck that drained out.

In my first formal coaching engagement, my coach asked me to spend time connecting my mind to my body. I made a commitment to mindfully go through a specific set of stretches each day. The week I committed to do this daily, I followed through for one day. So I decided that the stretching practice wasn't the one for me, and instead I elected to sit still for one minute each afternoon. I followed through on this practice all of three times over two weeks, while berating myself for lack of self-discipline. With more patience, persistence, and grace than I could offer myself, my coach held me to my commitment. It was exhausting and frustrating to fail day after day. But had my coach not encouraged me to continue searching for a mind-body practice, I would not have been frustrated enough to look for a deeper explanation. When I was truly at wit's end, I was ready to see the truth: I don't lack discipline; rather, I struggle with a deeply embedded belief that others' needs and desires come before my own. This revelation reframed my coaching goals and opened the door to many breakthrough conversations.

When Daniel shared the idea for this book with me, I was astounded that such a book didn't already exist. Given the investment that individuals and organizations make in coaching, and the impact that coaching can have at individual, team, and organizational levels, it just makes sense to give our clients every resource at our disposal to help them get the most out of their coaching engagement.

In the past, I would have said, "Good for you; great idea!" –and think, "I wish I could do something like that." My authorship of this book is a powerful testament to what can happen when we embody the power of coaching. My own coach has helped me recognize my worth and make bold requests to offer the value I bring. I was surprised at how easily my mind went from, "Good for you," to, "I could contribute to that!" –and even more surprised to find myself saying, "Can I co-author that with you?"

Each of us has encountered at least one shift that can change the trajectory of our life. Coaching helps us discover what is possible; it helps us start to see the fruits of the shifts we make in leadership and in life. What are the shifts you're after? Go get them!

Learn more about Cary at www.creatingopenspace.com.

Made in the USA
Middletown, DE
04 October 2015